The Compound Words
7,000 Compound and Hyphenated Words

Over 5,000 compound words and 2,000 hyphenated words are isolated in this book, grouped alphabetically, colored, and prepared for adults and children to read and learn. For sample lessons and much more, visit us at SpellingRules.com

Important Notes	III
A in 106 compound words, as in **art**work	1
A- in 29 hyphenated words, as in **attorney**-at-law	3
B in 486 compound words, as in **back**ground	5
B- in 89 hyphenated words, as in **blue**-collar	14
C in 413 compound words, as in **can**not	18
C- in 115 hyphenated words as, in **cross**-cultural	26
D in 169 compound words, as in **down**stairs	30
D- in 78 hyphenated words, as in **daughter**-in-law	33
E in 85 compound words, as in **easy**going	36
E- in 16 hyphenated words, as in **entry**-level	38
F in 368 compound words, as in **free**thinker	40
F- in 122 hyphenated words, as in **face**-to-face	47
G in 193 compound words, as in **grand**mother	51
G- in 58 hyphenated words, as in **good**-looking	55
H in 379 +150 additional compound words, as in **heart**breaking	58
H- in 145 + 145 additional hyphenated words, as in **hands**-on	65
I in 44 + 170 additional words compound words, as in **inter**change	69
I- in 25 hyphenated words, as in **ill**-mannered	70
J in 43 compound words, as in **juke**box	72
J- in 18 hyphenated words, as in **jack**-of-all-trades	73
K in 39 compound words, as in **key**board	75
K- in 16 hyphenated words, as in **know**-it-all	76
L in 168 compound words, as in **life**guard	78
L- in 64 hyphenated words, as in **leading**-edge	82
M in 158 compound words, as in **mid**summer	84
M- in 69 hyphenated words, as in **many**-sided	87

I

The Compound Words by Camilia Sadik

N in **103 + 700** compound words, as in **new**comer — 90
N- in **40** hyphenated words, as in **non**-American — 92

O in **247** compound words, as in **on**going — 94
O- in **63** hyphenated words, as in **off**-the-record — 97

P in **187** compound words, as in **play**ground — 100
P- in **88** hyphenated words, as in **part**-time — 104

Q in **9** compound words, as in **quarter**back — 107
Q- in **4** hyphenated words, as in **quick**-tempered — 107

R in **97** compound words, as in **rust**proof — 108
R- in **55** hyphenated words, as in **right**-wing — 110

S in **443** compound words, as in **school**mate — 113
S- in **241** hyphenated words, as in **short**-term — 121

T in **164** compound words, as in **time**saver — 127
T- in **80** hyphenated words, as in **tax**-exempt — 130

U in **119** compound words, as in **up**bringing — 133
U- in **6** hyphenated words, as in **under**-the-counter — 134

V in **14** compound words, as in **view**point — 136
V- in **1** hyphenated word as in **vice**-president — 136

W in **216** compound words, as in **work**force — 137
W- in **59** hyphenated words, as in **world**-famous — 141

Y in **15** compound words, as in **your**self — 144
Y- in **6** hyphenated words, as in **year**-round — 144

Z in **7** compound words, as in **zoo**keeper — 145
Z- in **4** compound words, as in **zero**-rated — 145

About the author Camilia Sadik and her other phonics-based spelling books — 147

For free sample lessons that teach the spelling of hundreds of words instantly, visit

SpellingRules.com

Important Notes

The Compound Words is a workbook for learning over 5,000 compound words and 2,000 hyphenated words. The 7,000 words in this book are grouped alphabetically, colored, and prepared for children and adults to simply read and learn their spelling. For instance, 106 compound words and 29 hyphenated words that begin with an "a" and listed on three pages.

Learning these words is fun and easy. You will learn most of them by simply looking at them. If you wish to memorize the spelling of hundreds of words at a time, you will need to read them aloud as many times as needed until you memorize their spelling.

What is a compound word?

As in "**text**book" and as in "**now**a**days**," a compound word is one word, composed of two or more other words. The following words are examples of some compound words:

cannot	**border**line	**how**ever
anyone	**any**thing	**every**thing
someone	**where**as	**what**ever
herself	**through**out	**break**through
keyboard	**lap**top	**down**load
goodbye	**finger**print	**fire**place
freeway	**after**noon	**air**plane
artwork	**back**ward	**business**man
birthday	**brain**wash	**now**a**days**

What is a hyphenated word?

A hyphenated word is a word made of the two or more words that are separated by hyphens, as in **self**-**esteem** and **step**-**by**-**step**. Usually, a noun follows a hyphenated word, as in "**down**-**to**-**earth** person" and, as in "**first**-**class** service."

all-out	**double**-click	**attorney**-at-law
carry-out	**back**-and-forth	**back**-to-back
down-the-line	**day**-to-day	**door**-to-door
empty-handed	**first**-class	**free**-for-all
full-time	**part**-time	**face**-to-face
hit-and-run	**have**-not	**ill**-natured

III

The Compound Words by Camilia Sadik

father-in-law   **know**-it-all   **like**-minded
out-of-order   **right**-handed   **left**-wing
run-down   **self**-help   **short**-term
simple-minded   **top**-notch   **user**-friendly

Examples of nouns preceded by a hyphenated word:

door-to-door salesman   **empty-handed** guest
full-time employment   **face-to-face** interview
high-class society   **six-member** committee
king-sized bed   **letter-size** page
low-keyed lady   **like-minded** people
left-handed artist   **run-down** apartments
round-table talks   **second-degree** burn
self-help workbook   **short-term** assignment
simple-minded fellow   **English-speaking** people
top-notch school   **time-saving** equipment
300-page book   **forty-four** dollars

Hyphenated Numbers

Numbers between 21 and 99 are hyphenated, as in **twenty**-**one**, **thirty**-**seven**, **fifty**-**three**, **sixty**-**eight**, and all the way to **ninety**-**nine**. Furthermore, numbers from "one to nine" must be spelled out as in, one boy, two girls, three houses, four men, five women, six books, seven trees, eight stars, nine cups. Either **10** boys or **ten** boys is correct, **11** girls or **eleven** girls is also correct.

twenty-one ☞to **twenty**-nine   **thirty**-one ☞to **thirty**-nine
forty-one ☞to **forty**-nine   **fifty**-one ☞to **fifty**-nine
sixty-one ☞to **sixty**-nine   **seventy**-one ☞to **seventy**-nine
eighty-one ☞to **eighty**-nine   **ninety**-one ☞to **ninety**-nine

A

after

afterbirth   **after**care   **after**life
afterworld   **after**image   **after**effect
aftermath   **after**shock   **after**taste
afterglow   **after**piece   **after**thought
aftershave   **after**time   **after**noon
aftermarket   **after**most   **after**damp
afterdeck   **after**burner   **after**ward
afterwards

air

airmail   **air**plane   **air**port
airline   **air**mobile   **air**craft
anti**air**craft   **air**ship   **air**fare
airborne   **air**brush   **air**burst
airfield   **air**flow   **air**foil
airframe   **air**bag   **air**brake
airbladder   **air**frame   **air**freight
airglow   **air**head   **air**play
airsickness   **air**less   **air**space
airstrip   **air**tight   **air**wave
airworthy

The Compound Words by Camilia Sadik

any

anybody   **any**one   **any**how
anyway   **any**ways   **any**more
anyplace   **any**thing   **any**time
anywhere   **any**wise

arm

armpit   **arm**hole   **arm**let
armrest

arch

archbishop   **arch**deacon   **arch**diocese
archduke   **arch**ducal   **arch**duchess
archduchy   **arch**way   **archer**fish

aweless   **awe**struck   **awe**some

anglesite   **angle**worm
alongshore   **along**side
alderwomen   **alder**man
alewife   **ale**house
almshouse   **alms**man
allover   **all**spice
applesauce   **apple**jack
assemblyman   **assembly**woman
artwork   **art**less
arrowhead   **arrow**root

A

artilleryman   **angel**fish   **alley**way
areaway   **aroma**therapy   **author**ship
addlebrained

A-

all-day   **all**-embracing   **all**-friend
all-important   **all**-inclusive   **all**-or-nothing
all-out   **all**-powerful   **all**-purpose
all-around   **all**-star   **all**-time
all-terrain   **all**-right   **al**right, **all** right

air-to-air   **air**-traffic control
apple-pie   **apple**-polish

across-the-board   **aide**-de-camp   **airy**-fairy
almond-eyed   **around**-the-clock   **attorney**-at-law
accented-lantern

⬆ Practice of all the above words: Read the above words aloud slowly as many times as needed until you memorize their spelling.

The Compound Words by Camilia Sadik

✎ Make **three** copies of this page to copy the above compound & hyphenated words that begin with an **A**. Look at each word before you begin to copy it; do not try to guess its spelling:

B

back

backache	**back**bone	**back**breaking
backrest	**back**side	**back**stage
backyard	**back**ground	**back**space
backseat	**back**stairs	**back**pack
backstop	**back**fire	**back**lash
backbeat	**back**bench	**back**light
backbite	**back**board	**back**court
backcross	**back**date	**back**drop
backfield	**back**fill	**back**flow
backgammon	**back**hand	**back**hoe
backlist	**back**log	**back**saw
backscatter	**back**slapping	**back**slash
backsplash	**back**slide	**back**spin
backstay	**back**stitch	**back**order
backroom	**back**stroke	**back**swept
backswimmer	**back**sword	**back**track
backup	**back**ward	**back**wards
backwash	**back**water	**back**woods
backwoodsman		

black

blackberry	**black**bird	**black**board
blackbody	**Black**burn	**black**cap

blackdamp   blackfish   blackface
blackhead   blackheart   blackleg
blackjack   blacklist   blackmail
blackout   blacksmith   Blackstone
blackthorn   blacktop   Blackwell
Blackwood

bed

bedroom   bedtime   bedbug
bedchamber   bedclothes   bedspread
bedspring   bedfellow   bedrock
bedroll   bedside   bedfast
bedpan   bedpost   bedridden
bedsore   bedstead   bedstraw
bedwetting

band

bandbox   bandleader   bandmaster
bandstand   bandwagon   bandwidth

bar

barkeeper   bartender   barman
barmaid   barware   barhop
barrack   barroom

bee

beebread   beehive   beeline
beekeeper   beechnut

B

ball
ballplayer **ball**game **ball**park
ballroom **ball**point

big
bighead **Big**foot **big**hearted
bighorn **big**wig **big**mouth
bigmouthed

bat
batfish **bat**fowl **bat**man
batwing

bill
billboard **bill**bug **bill**fish
billfold **bill**hook

bird
birdhouse **bird**lime **bird**man
birdseed

birth
birthday **birth**place **birth**mark
birthrate **birth**root **birth**right
birthstone

blood
bloodroot **blood**shed **blood**shot
bloodstain **blood**stock **blood**stone
bloodstream **blood**sucker **blood**thirsty
bloodworm

All the Compound Words by Camilia Sadik

blue

bluebeard · blueberry · bluebird
bluebonnet · bluebottle · bluefish
bluebook · bluegill · bluegrass
bluenose · blueprint · bluestem
bluestocking · bluestone · bluetongue
blueweed

blow

Blowfish · blowgun · blowhole
blowout · blowup · blowpipe
blowtorch

book

bookstore · bookbinding · bookcase
bookend · bookkeeping · bookmaker
bookmarker · bookmobile · bookplate
bookrack · bookshelf · bookstand
bookseller · bookstall · bookshop
bookworm

boot

bootblack · bootjack · bootlick
bootlace · bootless · bootleg
bootstrap · bootblack

bow

bowhead · bowfin · bowknot
bowline · bowman · bowsprit

bowstring   bowwow

brain
brainchild   brainwash   brainless
brainpan   brainpower   brainsick
brainstem   brainstorm   brainteaser

bread
breadbasket   breadbox   breadboard
breadcrumbs   breadfruit   breadroot
breadstuff   breadwinner

break
breakaway   breakdown   breakeven
breakfast   breakfront   breakneck
breakpoint   breakthrough   breakout
breakup   breakwater

breast
breastbone   breastplate   breaststroke
breastwork   breastfeed   breastfed

broad
broadcast   broadcasting   broadcloth
broadleaf   broadleaved   broadloom
broadside   broadsheet   broadsword
Broadway   broadminded

buck

buckboard   **buck**eye   **buck**saw
buckshot   **buck**skin   **buck**thorn
bucktooth

bull

bulldog   **bull**bat   **bull**doze
bulldozer   **bull**fight   **bull**finch
bullfrog   **bull**head   **bull**headed
bullhorn   **bull**necked   **bull**whip

business

businesslike   **business**people   **business**person
businessman   **business**woman

butter

butterball   **butter**milk   **butter**weed
buttercup   **butter**nut   **butter**scotch
butterfat   **butter**fingers   **butter**fish
butterfly

button

buttonbush   **button**hole   **button**hook
buttonwood

by

bygone   **by**law   **by**line
byname   **by**pass   **by**play
bystander   **by**way   **by**word

B

bush
bushbuck · bushfire · bushman
bushmaster · bushranger · bushwhack
bushwhacker

bare
barefoot · bareback · bareheaded
barelegged

bag
bagman · bagpipe · bagwig
bagworm

bank
bankbook · bankroll · bankrupt
bankruptcy

base
baseball · baseboard · baseless
baseline

bath
bathroom · bathhouse · bathtub
bathrobe

beef
beefeater · beefsteak · beefwood
beefcake

boat
boatlift · boatload · boatman
boatswain

All the Compound Words by Camilia Sadik

bone
bonefish   **bone**head   **bone**set
bonesetter

bottle
bottlebrush   **bottle**neck   **bottle**nose

box
boxboard   **box**car   **box**thorn
boxwood

brick
brickbat   **brick**laying   **brick**work
brickyard

brown
brownbag   **brown**nose   **brown**out
brownstone

beachfront   **beach**head   **beach**wear
beanbag   **bean**pole   **bean**stalk
bearbaiting   **bear**berry   **bear**skin
bitternut   **bitter**root   **bitter**sweet
boardroom   **board**sailing   **board**walk
bombshell   **bomb**proof   **bomb**sight
bondholder   **bond**maid   **bond**man
breechblock   **breech**loader   **breech**cloth
broomstick   **broom**corn   **broom**rape
brushwood   **brush**work   **brush**fire

B

buyback	**buy**off	**buy**out
busboy	**bus**girl	**bus**man
bughouse	**bug**bear	**bug**bane
buyback	**buy**off	**buy**out
busboy	**bus**girl	**bus**man

badlands **bad**mouth
bailout **bails**man
baldheaded **bald**pate
bargeman **barge**board
barnburner **barn**storm
basketball **basket**work
battlefield **battle**ship
beforehand **before**time
borderline **border**land
boyfriend **boy**hood
breathless **breath**taking
bottomless **bottom**most
bridgework **bridge**head
briarwood **briar**root
broadax **broad**band
bridegroom **brides**maid
bullyboy **bully**rag
bunkhouse **bunk**mate
burnout **burn**sides

busybody   busywork

bandsman   barleycorn   barnyard
barbershop   basswood   batsman
beeswax   behindhand   betweenwhiles
bikeway   bindweed   Birdseye
bollworm   boltrope   bondsman
boardinghouse   boathouse   boondocks
botfly   boundless   borehole
bowerbird   brassbound   breadthways
breezeway   brewpub   briefcase
brimstone   brinkmanship   bristletail
brittlebush   bugleweed   brokenhearted
browbeat   budworm   brotherhood
bulletproof   bumblebee   bunchberry
buzzword   buckwheat   buildup
butcherbird

B-

back-load   back-pedal   back-back-and-forth
back-check   back-to-back

ball-peen hammer ball-and-claw   ball-ball-and-foot

B

black-and-blue   black-and-tan   black-and-white
black-hearted   black-market   black-tailed

blow-by   blow-by-blow   blow-dry
blow-dryer   blow-hard

blue-collar   blue-curls   blue-eyed grass
blue-green algae blue-pencil   blue-rinse
blue-rinsed   blue-sky

by-and-by   by-blow   by-election
by-product

battle-ax   battle-scarred
bed-sitter   bed-and-breakfast
bee-eater   bee-stung
bird-dog   birds-eye
brand-new   brand-name
breast-beating   breast-feed
broad-brush   broad-spectrum
Brown-shirt   brown-tail moth

15

All the Compound Words by Camilia Sadik

bulls-eye   **bull**-whip

bachelor-button	**bandy**-legged	**bang**-up
Band-Aid	**barrow**-boy	**base**-pairing
basket-of-gold	**beam**-ends	**beggar**-sticks
behind-the-scene	**big**-ticket	**billet**-doux
birth-control pill	**blood**-red	**bloody**-minded
bone-dry	**born**-again	**brain**-dead
brass-collar	**bread**-and-butter	**break**-in
bred-n the-bone	**bright**-eyed	**broken**-down
brother-in-law	**brown**-eyed	**brush**-off
back-and-wing	**bug**-eyed	**build**-up
built-up	**bumper**-to-bumper	**bum**-rush
bust-up	**buttoned**-up	**bottom**-down
butcher's-broom	**butter**-and-eggs	**bye**-bye
baby-sit		

⬆ Practice of all the above words: Read the above words aloud slowly as many times as needed until you memorize their spelling.

✍ Make **12** copies of this page to copy the above compound & hyphenated words that begin with a **B**. Look at each word before you begin to copy it; do not try to guess its spelling:

C

candle

candlelight   **candle**lit   **candle**power
candlenut   **candle**pin   **candle**berry
candlestick   **candle**wick   **candle**wood

care

carefree   **care**giver   **care**less
caretaker   **care**worn

car

carfare   **car**go   **car**hop
carjacking   **car**load   **car**maker
carwash   **car**sick   **car**port
carrack   **car**mine   **car**nation

cat

catnap   **cat**nip   **cat**like
catmint   **cat**fish   **cat**walk

check

checkbook   **check**list   **check**mate
checkout   **check**up   **check**point
checkrein   **check**room

C

child

childbearing   childbirth   childhood
childlike   childbed   childproof

China

Chinatown   Chinaman   chinaberry
chinaware

clothes

clothesline   clotheshorse   clothespin
clothespress

cock

cocktail   cockboat   cockcrow
cockroach   cockeye   cockeyed
cockfight   cockhorse   cockloft
cockpit   cockshy   cocksure
cocksfoot

copy

copybook   copyboy   copycat
copygirl   copyhold   copyholder
copyright   copyreader   copywriter
copywriting   copyeditor

corn

cornball   corncob   cornhusk
cornfield   cornflakes   cornflower

The Compound Words by Camilia Sadik

cornmeal   **corn**row   **corn**starch
cornstalk

cotton
cottonmouth   **cotton**seed   **cotton**tail
cottonweed   **cotton**wood

country
countryman   **country**woman   **country**side
countryseat

court
courthouse   **court**room   **court**yard
courtship   **court**side

cow
cowbell   **cow**bane   **cow**pox
cowberry   **cow**pea   **cow**bird
cowfish   **cow**herd   **cow**boy
cowgirl   **cow**man   **cow**catcher
cowpuncher   **cow**hide   **cow**poke
cowhand   **cow**lick   **cow**shed
cowslip

cross
crossbar   **cross**beam   **cross**bones
crossbow   **cross**breed   **cross**bred
crosscourt   **cross**current   **cross**cutting

C

crossfire **cross**hatch **cross**head
crossjack **cross**over **cross**patch
crosspiece **cross**road **cross**ruff
crosstree **cross**walk **cross**way
crossword puzzle **cross**wind

cut

cutaway **cut**back **cut**off
cutout **cut**over **cut**throat
cutup **cut**water **cut**work
cutworm

camp

campfire **camp**ground **camp**site
campstool

case

caseharden **case**load **case**mate
casework

center

centerfold **center**board **center**line
centerpiece

chair

chairperson **chair**man **chair**woman
chairlift

The Compound Words by Camilia Sadik

char
charbroil   **char**coal   **char**lock
charwoman

cheese
cheeseburger   **cheese**cake   **cheese**cloth
cheeseparing

choke
chokeberry   **choke**cherry   **choke**damp
chokepoint

church
churchman   **church**woman   **church**warden
churchyard

coast
coastguard   **coast**guardsman   **coast**land
coastline   **coast**ward   **coast**wise

clock
clocklike   **clock**maker   **clock**wise
clockwork

coffee
coffeecake   **coffee**house   **coffee**maker
coffeepot

C
crack

crackdown **crack**brain **crack**pot
crackup

crowbar **crow**berry **crow**foot
cabdriver **cab**man **cab**stand
cablecast **cable**gram **cable**vision
cameraperson **camera**man **camera**woman
cannot **can**to **can**ton
cardboard **card**holder **card**sharp
chapbook **chap**fallen **chap**lain
cheerlead **cheer**leader **cheer**less
classmate **class**room **class**less
clearheaded **clear**wing **clear**water
colorcast **color**fast **color**less
congressperson **congress**woman **congress**man
corkscrew **cork**board **cork**wood
cornerback **corner**stone **corner**wise
crabmeat **crab**stick **crab**wise
craftsperson **crafts**man **crafts**woman

cabinetmaker **cabinet**work
camelhair **camel**back
carpetbag **carpet**weed

carryall	**carry**over
castaway	**cast**off
cellmate	**cell**block
chalkboard	**chalk**stone
chambermaid	**chamber**lain
cheapjack	**cheap**skate
chessboard	**chess**man
chickpea	**chick**weed
chipboard	**chip**munk
chiliburger	**chili**dog
choirboy	**choir**master
Christmastime	**Christmas**tide
cityscape	**city**wide
clamshell	**clam**worm
clansman	**clans**woman
clapboard	**clap**trap
clergyman	**clergy**woman
cloudburst	**cloud**land
clubhouse	**club**foot
coatdress	**coat**room
cobweb	**cob**nut
codfish	**cod**piece
comeback (n.)	**come**down
commonweal	**common**wealth
companionship	**companion**way

C

coneflower · conenose
containerboard · containership
cookhouse · cookware
coonhound · coonskin
copperhead · copperplate
coralberry · coralline
cordless · cordwood
councilman · councilwoman
countdown · countable
crankcase · crankshaft
crawdad · crawfish
crookback · crookneck
curbside · curbstone
cuttlebone · cuttlefish
closefisted · closefitting
cabbageworm · candytuft · cableway
cachepot · cakewalk · callboy
canebrake · cankerworm · cannonball
canvasback · capeskin · caplet
caveman · cartwheel · cashbook
cattleman · causeway · cavalryman
censorship · championship · charterhouse
chatterbox · chapfallen · cheekbone
cherrystone · checkerboard · chestnut
chickenpox · chitchat · chinbone

chockfull
claymore
clingstone
cloudberry
coachman
colicroot
coldhearted
courseware
cradlesong
crayfish
crestfallen
crisscross
crybaby
cudweed
cybernation

chucklehead
cleanup
clipboard
cloverleaf
coattail
collarbone
coolheaded
coverall
crapshoot
crazyweed
crewman
cropland
cryptanalysis
currycomb

clampdown
clearinghouse
cloakroom
clueless
cobblestone
colorblind
copout
crackleware
crashworthiness
creditworthy
crewmen
crownpiece
crystalline
customhouse

C-

close-by
close-loop
close-knit

close-cropped
close-grained

close-
close-end
close-hauled

cross-action
cross-checker

cross-bearer
cross-country

cross-
cross-check
cross-culture

cross-cultural **cross**-dress **cross**-examine
cross-eye **cross**-fertilization **cross**-fertile
cross-file **cross**-garnet **cross**-index
cross-legged **cross**-link **cross**-pollinate
cross-nation **cross**-purpose **cross**-question
cross-react **cross**-reaction **cross**-reference
cross-resistance **cross**-stitch **cross**-tolerance
cross-train

cut-
cut-and-dried **cut**-and-paste **cut**-grass
cut-in **cut**-rate

call-
call-back **call**-board **call**-in
call-up

clean-
clean-cut **clean**-shaven **clean**-handed
clean-limed

clear-cut **clear**-eyed **clear**-sighted
cock-a-doodle-doo **cocks**-of-the-rock **cock**-a-hoop

cable-laid **cable**-ready
carbon-date **carbon**-acid gas

The Compound Words by Camilia Sadik

carry-on **carry**-out
chicken-hearted **chicken**-livered
conscience-stricken **consciousness**-raising
court-bouillon **court**-martial
crow's-foot **crow's**-nest
crash-dive **crash**-land

camera-shy **can**-do **cap**-a-pipe
carvel-built **cash**-and-carry **cat's**-eye
catty-corner **cave**-in **C**-clamp
CD-ROM **chain**-smoke **chance**-medley
channel-surf **check**-in **chop**-chop
chow-chow **chuck**-full **chug**-a-lug
chute-the-chute **city**-state **clap**-out
cliff-hanger **civic**-minded **clinker**-built
clip-on **cloak**-and-dagger **closed**-door
cloud-cuckoo-land **cloven**-footed **coast**-to-coast
cold-blooded **color**-code **come**-hither
command-driven **comparison**-shop **crack**-barrel
country-dance **counselor**-at-law **cram**-full
crane-bill **crop**-eared **crystal**-clear
cure-all **custom**-built

⬆ Practice of all the above words: Read the above words aloud slowly as many times as needed until you memorize their spelling.

C

✍ Make **11** copies of this page to copy the above compound & hyphenated words that begin with a **C**. Look at each word before you begin to copy it; do not try to guess its spelling:

The Compound Words by Camilia Sadik

D

day

daylight   **day**time   **day**break
daydream   **day**long   **day**bed
daybook   **day**fly   **day**side
daystar

dead

deadline   **dead**beat   **dead**bolt
deadeye   **dead**fall   **dead**head
deadlight   **dead**lock   **dead**pan
deadwood

dish

dishwasher   **dish**rag   **dish**towel
dishpan   **dish**water   **dish**cloth
dishpan

dog

dogberry   **dog**cart   **dog**catcher
dogface   **dog**fight   **dog**fish
doghouse   **dog**leg   **dog**nap
dogsled   **dog**tooth   **dog**watch
dogwood

door

doorbell   **door**jamb   **door**keeper
doorknob   **door**man   **door**mat
doornail   **door**post   **door**sill

doorstep   **door**stop   **door**way
dooryard

down
downbeat   **down**cast   **down**draft
downfall   **down**field   **down**grade
downhaul   **down**hearted   **down**hill
downlink   **down**load   **down**play
downpour   **down**range   **down**right
downriver   **down**scale   **down**shift
downside   **down**size   **down**slide
downspin   **down**spout   **down**stage
downstairs   **down**state   **down**stream
downswing   **down**tick   **down**time
downtown   **down**trend   **down**trodden
downturn   **down**ward   **down**wind

draw
drawback   **draw**bar   **draw**bridge
drawknife   **draw**shave   **draw**tube

drum
drumbeat   **drum**fire   **drum**head
drumstick

The Compound Words by Camilia Sadik

duck
duckbill   **duck**board   **duck**pins
ducktail   **duck**weed

death
deathbed   **death**blow   **death**trap
deathwatch

dumb
dumbbell   **dumb**found   **dumb**struck
dumbwaiter

dust
dustbin   **dust**pan   **dust**man
dustup

doubleheader   **double**speak   **double**think
dragline   **drag**onfly   **drag**rope
dreamland   **dream**less   **dream**time
dairyman   **dairy**woman   **dairy**maid
deerhound   **deer**skin   **deer**stalker
desktop   **desk**bound   **desk**man
dewberry   **dew**claw   **dew**lap
darkroom   **dark**some
dateless   **date**line
dinnertime   **dinner**ware
draftsman   **drafts**person

D

driveline
driveway
droplight
dropout
dyestuff
dyewood

dartboard
dashboard
dauntless
deejay
dessertspoon
devilwood
diamondback
dieback
dimwit
doomsday
doomsayer
drainpipe
dressmaker
driftwood
drillmaster
dugout
Dutchman
dunghill

D-

double-click
double-space
double-
double-cross
double-dealing
double-acting
double-lock
double-park
double-barreled
double-book
double-breasted
double-chick
double-decker
double-digit
double-dipping
double-edged
double-faced
double-hung
double-jointed
double-quick
double-reed
double-ring
double-stop
double-talk
double-tongue
double-time

down-
down-and-dirty
down-and-out
down-at-heel
down-bow
down-home
down-the-line
down-to-earth
down-out

deep-dyed   **deep**-freeze   **deep**-fry
deep-rooted   **deep**-sea   **deep**-seated
deep-six

drive-by   **drive**-in   **drive**-through
drive-up

drop-dead   **drop**-in   **drop**-off
drop-out

dry-as-dust   **dry**-eyed   **dry**-roasted
dry-point

deaf-and-dumb   **deaf**-blind   **deaf**-mute
day-to-day   **day**-tripper
dead-end   **dead**-on
do-it-yourself   **do**-or-die

daughter-in-law   **daylight**-savings   **dewy**-eyed
dark-field time   **dial**-up   **die**-off
diesel-electric   **doo**-wop   **doe**-eyed
door-to-door   **dressing**-down   **dried**-up
drip-dry   **dumping**-ground   **D**-day
dyed-in-the-wool

⬆ Practice of all the above words: Read the above words aloud slowly as many times as needed until you memorize their spelling.

✎ Make **six** copies of this page to copy the above compound & hyphenated words that begin with a **D**. Look at each word before you begin to copy it; do not try to guess its spelling:

E

every

everything everywhere everybody
everyone everyman everyday
everyplace

ear

earache eardrop eardrum
earflap earlap earless
earmark earmuff earphone
earpiece earplug earshot
earsplitting

earth

earthborn earthbound earthlight
earthmover earthnut earthquake
earthshaking earthrise earthshine
earthstar earthward earthwork
earthworm

eye

eyeball eyelashes eyebrows
eyelid eyebolt eyebright
eyecup eyedropper eyeglasses
eyehole eyelet eyelift
eyeliner eyepiece eyeshade

E

eyeshot   **eye**sight   **eye**sore
eyespot   **eye**stalk   **eye**strain
eyetooth   **eye**wash   **eye**wear
eyewink   **eye**witness

egg

eggbeater   **egg**cup   **egg**head
eggshell   **egg**plant

end

endless   **end**most   **end**point
endways

everlasting   **ever**green   **ever**more
extraordinary   **extra**curricular   **extra**marital
eastbound   **east**ward
edgewise   **edge**ways

easternmost   **easy**going   **eight**fold
elsewhere   **English**woman   **entry**way
expressway

Tthe Compound Words by Camilia Sadik

E-

end-all   **end**-arch   **end**-**end**-blown

end-stopped

eye-catcher   **eye**-popper   **eye**-only

empty-handed   **empty**-headed

earth-shattering   **eighteen**-wheeler /   **18**-wheeleran
either-or situation   **entry**-level   **even**-tempered
evil-minded   **eyeball**-to-eyeball

⬆ Practice of all the above words: Read the above words aloud slowly as many times as needed until you memorize their spelling.

✍ Make **three** copies of this page to copy the above compound & hyphenated words that begin with the letter **E**. Look at each word before you begin to copy it; do not try to guess its spelling:

The Compound Words by Camilia Sadik

F

face
facecloth
facedown
faceless
facelift
faceplate

feather
featherbedding
featherbrain
featheredge
featherhead
featherstitch
featherweight

finger
fingerboard
fingerprint
fingerprinting
fingernail
fingertip

fire
firearm
fireball
fireboat
firebomb
firebox
firebrand
firebrat
firebreak
firebrick
firebug
firecracker
firedamp
firedog
firedrake
firefighter
firefly
fireguard
firehouse
firelight
firelock
fireman
fireplace
fireplug
firepower
fireproof
fireproofing
fireside
firestorm
firethorn
firetrap
firewater
fireweed
firewood
firework

F

flash

flashbulb   flashcard   flashcube
flashgun   flashlight   flashover
flashpoint

flat

flatbed   flatboat   flatbread
flatcar   flatfish   flatfoot
flatfooted   flatiron   flatland
flattop   flatware   flatwork
flatworm

fly

flyaway   flyblow   flyblown
flyboy   flyby   flycatcher
flyleaf   flyover   flypaper
flyspeck   flytrap   flyway
flyweight   flywheel

foot

football   footbath   footboard
footboy   footbridge   footcloth
footfall   footgear   foothill
foothold   footless   footlight
footlocker   footloose   footman
footmark   footnote   footpace
footpad   footpath   footprint

The Compound Words by Camilia Sadik

footrace	footrest	footrope
footslog	footsore	footstalk
footstep	footstone	footstool
footwall	footway	footwear
footwork		

fore

forebrain	forecast	forecastle
foreclose	foreclosure	forecourt
forefather	forefeel	forefend
forefinger	forefoot	forefront
foregather	forego	foregoing
foregone	foreground	foregut
forehand	forehanded	forehead
forejudge	foreknow	foreknowledge
forelady	foreland	foreleg
forelock	foreman	foremast
foremilk	foremost	foremother
forename	forenamed	forenoon
foreordain	forepart	forepaw
foreperson	foreplay	forequarter
forereach	forerun	forerunner
foresaid	foresail	foresee
foreseeable	foreshadow	foresheet
foreshock	foreshore	foreshorten
foreshow	foreside	foresight

F

foreskin
forestay
foretaste
forethoughtful
forewent
foreword

forespeak
forestaysail
foretell
foretime
forewing
foreworn

forestall
foreswear
forethought
foretoken
forewoman

for

forever
forgo
formalwear
forsooth
forthcoming
forward

forevermore
forkball
formfitting
forswear
forthright
forwards

forgather
forklift
formless
forsworn
forthwith
forwent

free

freebase
freebooter
freefall
freehanded
freeholder
freeman
freestone
freeware
freewill

freeboard
freeborn
freeform
freehearted
freelance
freemasonry
freestyle
freeway

freeboot
freewoman
freehand
freehold
freeload
freestanding
freethinker
freewheel

43

The Compound Words by Camilia Sadik

fish

fishnet   **fish**plate   **fish**pond
fishtail   **fish**wife

fox

foxfire   **fox**glove   **fox**hole
foxhound   **fox**tail

farm

farmhouse   **farm**land   **farm**stead
farmyard

fall

fallback   **fall**fish   **fall**off
fallout

fair

fairground   **fair**lead   **fair**way
fairyland

fan

fanfare   **fan**fold   **fan**light
fantail

flea

fleabag   **flea**bite   **flea**pit
fleawort

flag

flagman   **flag**on   **flag**pole
flagship

44

F

flood
floodgate floodlight floodwater
floodway

four
fourfold fourhanded fourscore
foursquare

frog
frogeye frogfish froghopper
frogman

front
frontrunner frontward frontline
frontload

faraway farfetched farsighted
filmgoer filmmaker filmstrip
feedback feedbox feedstuff
fiberboard fiberfill fiberglass

fatback fathead
faultfinder faultless
fearless fearsome
fastback fastball
ferryman ferryboat
fiddlehead fiddlestick

The Compound Words by Camilia Sadik

fieldstone	fieldwork	
floorboard	floorwalker	
firstborn	firsthand	
flameproof	flamethrower	
fogbound	fogbow	
foldaway	foldout	
folkmoot	folkway	
Frenchman	Frenchwoman	
freshman	freshwater	
fruitcake	fruitless	
fussbudget	fusspot	
farthermost	fatherland	
faithless	failsafe	fadeout
falsehood	fancywork	farewell
fellowman	figurehead	filename
firmware	fisherman	fivefold
flapdoodle	flaxseed	fleshpots
flextime	flimflam	flintlock
floatplane	flophouse	flowerpot
flowstone	foamflower	foeman
foodstuff	foolproof	forestland
fountainhead	framework	fretwork
frostbite	fullback	funnyman
furbearer	futureless	

F-

far-
far-flung
far-gone
far-off
far-out
far-point
far-reaching

first-
first-class
first-degree burn
first-generation
first-rate
first-in
first-out
first-string

foot-
foot-candle
foot-and-mouth disease
foot-Lambert
foot-pond
foot-pound-second
foot-roundel
foot-ton

fore-
fore-check
fore-topgallant
fore-top-most
fore-top-sail

four-
four-by-four/4 x 4
four-dimensional
four-eye
four-eyed
four-flush
four-o'clock
four-on-the-floor
four-star
four-way
four-wheel
fourth-class

The Compound Words by Camilia Sadik

free-

free-floating   free-for-all   free-living
free-range   free-spoken   free-swimming

full-

full-blooded   full-blown   full-bodied
full-bore   full-dress   full-fashioned
full-fledged   full-frontal   full-gainer
full-length   full-mouthed   full-scale
full-serves   full-size   full-sized
full-time

fly-

fly-by-night   fly-by-wire   fly-cast
fly-fish

fair-haired   fair-spoken   fair-trade
fast-food   fast-forward   fast-talk
follow-on   follow-up   follow-through

fat-soluble   fat-witted
face-off   face-to-face
field-strip   field-test
fine-drawn   fine-tooth
flame-out   flame-retardant

F

flash-forward   flash-freeze
floor-length   floor-through
forty-five   forty-niner
front-page   front-wheel drive
fund-raise   fund-raiser
fade-in   falling-out   false-hearted
fancy-free   fare-thee-well   father-in-law
feel-good   fee-splitting   fifty-fifty/50-50
fill-in   finger-pointing   fire-eater
fine-drawn   five-finger   flat-out
flea-bitten   flight-test   flip-flop
foreign-born   forget-me-not   forte-piano
fortune-teller   foul-up   fox-trot
frame-up   freeze-dry   French-fry

⬆ Practice of all the above words: Read the above words aloud slowly as many times as needed until you memorize their spelling.

The Compound Words by Camilia Sadik

✎ Make **11** copies of this page to copy the above compound & hyphenated words that begin with an **F**. Look at each word before you begin to copy it; do not try to guess its spelling:

G

glass
glassblowing   **glass**house   **glass**making
glassware   **glass**work   **glass**wort

gate
gatefold   **gate**house   **gate**keeper
gatepost   **gate**way

goal
goalkeeper   **goal**mouth   **goal**post
goaltender   **goal**tending

god
godchild   **god**daughter   **god**father
godmother   **god**parents   **god**son
godforsaken   **god**head   **god**less
godlike   **god**send   **god**wit

gold
goldbrick   **gold**finch   **gold**mine
goldsmith   **gold**stone

grand
grandparents   **grand**children   **grand**child

All the Compound Words by Camilia Sadik

grandkid   **grand**son   **grand**daughter
grandmother   **grand**ma   **gran**ny
grandfather   **grand**pa   **grand**dad
granddaddy   **grand**aunt   **grand**uncle
grandniece   **grand**nephew   **grand**stand

green
greenbelt   **green**back   **green**finch
greenfly   **green**gage   **green**grocer
greenheart   **green**horn   **green**house
greenmail   **green**room   **green**sand
greenshank   **green**stone   **green**sward
Greenwich Time

ground
groundbreaking   **ground**hog   **ground**skeeper
groundless   **ground**mass   **ground**nut
groundout   **ground**sheet   **ground**water
groundswell

gum
gumboil   **gum**boot   **gum**shoe
gumdrop   **gum**wood

G

gun

gunboat   **gun**cotton   **gun**fire
gunshot   **gun**flint   **gun**lock
gunman   **gun**metal   **gun**play
gunpoint   **gun**powder   **gun**running
gunship   **gun**slinger   **gun**smith
gunstock   **gun**wale

gang

gangbuster   **gang**land   **gang**plank
gangway

goat

goatherd   **goat**fish   **goat**skin
goatsucker

good

goodbye   **good**hearted   **good**will
goodwife

goose

gooseberry   **goose**foot   **goose**neck
gooseherd

All the Compound Words by Camilia Sadik

gray

graybeard   **gray**fish   **gray**lag
graymail

gasbag   **gas**light   **gas**works
grapefruit   **grape**shot   **grape**vine
gravedigger   **grave**yard   **grave**stone
guidebook   **guide**line   **guide**post

gearshift   **gear**wheel
gemstone   **gem**mated
gentleman   **gentle**folk
germfree   **germ**proof
getaway   **get**up
gingerbread   **ginger**snap
girlfriend   **girl**hood
giveaway   **give**back
gadabout   **gad**fly
grasshopper   **grass**land
gridlock   **grid**iron
greathearted   **great**coat
grillroom   **grill**work
guardroom   **guard**rail
gutbucket   **gut**less
gyroscope   **gyro**plane

greasewood **grease**paint

gagman **gall**stone **game**keeper
gamesmanship **glad**some **globe**trotter
goldenrod **g**host writer **gift**ware
gillyflower **goof**ball **grace**less
greyhound **grind**stone **grip**sack
gristmill **griddle**cake **grog**shop
groomsman **group**think **grub**stake
guesswork **guest**house **guards**man
guiltless **gunny**sack **gutter**snipe

G-

good-fellowship **good**-for-nothing **good**-
good-looker **good**-looking **good**-humored
good-sized **good**-tempered **good**-natured

go-
go-ahead **go**-between **go**-cart
go-devil **go**-getter **go**-no-go

55

get-go   **get**-together   **get**-up-and-go

green-eyed   **green**-winged teal   **green**-light

gas-guzzler   **gas**-operated

gavel-kind   **gavel**-to-gavel

gentleman-farmer   **gentleman**-at-arms

gentle-person   **gentle**-woman

gold-filled   **gold**-plated

goof-off   **goof**-up

great-aunt   **great**-nephew

gate-crasher   **gab**-toothed   **gee**-whiz

give-and-take   **glassy**-eyed   **gift**-wrap

gill-netter   **goggle**-eyed   **golden**-brown

goody-goody   **grant**-in-aid   **gravel**-blind

Greek-letter   **gross**-out   **grand**-effect

machine**grown**-up   **guilt**-trip   **gung**-ho

gun-shy   **gut**-winching   **gender**-specific

general-purpose

⬆ Practice of all the above words: Read the above words aloud slowly as many times as needed until you memorize their spelling.

✍ Make **six** copies of this page to copy the above compound & hyphenated words that begin with a **G**. Look at each word before you begin to copy it; do not try to guess its spelling:

H

hair

hairball
hairbrush
hairdresser
hairline
hairstreak

hairbreadth
haircut
hairstyle
hairpiece

haircloth
hairdo
hairstylist
hairsplitting

half

halfback
halftime
halfway

halfhearted
halftone

halfpenny
halftrack

hand

handbag
handbook
handcart
handcuff
handheld
handlebar
handmaiden
handrail
handshake
handstand
handwriting

handball
handbreadth
handclasp
handgrip
handhold
handmade
handout
handsaw
handsome
handwork

handbill
handcar
handcraft
handgun
handholding
handmaid
handpick
handset
handspring
handwrite

hard

hardback
hardbound
hardheaded

hardball
hardcover
hardhearted

hardboard
hardhack

hat

hatband
hatpin
haycock
hayrack
hayseed

hatbox
hatchback
hayloft
hayrick
haystack

hatcheck
hatchway
haymaker
hayride
haywire

head

headachy
headdress
headhunting
headlight
headlock
headmaster
headphone
headquarters
headsail
headman
headstand
headstrong
headway
headwork

headboard
headfirst
headland
headline
headlong
headmistress
headpiece
headrest
headset
headspring
headstock
headwaiter
headwind

headcheese
headgear
headless
headliner
headman
headmost
headpin
headroom
headship
headstall
headstone
headwaters
headword

The Compound Words by Camilia Sadik

heart

heartache heartbeat heartbreak
heartbreaker heartbreaking heartburn
heartfelt heartland heartless
heartrending heartsick heartstrings
heartthrob heartwarming heartwood

hell

hellbender hellbox hellcat
hellfire hellhole hellhound

hen

henbane henbit henceforth
hencoop henhouse henpeck

here

hereabout hereafter hereby
herein hereinafter hereinbefore
hereinto hereof hereon
hereto heretofore hereunder
hereupon herewith

high

highball highbinder highborn
highboy highchair highflier
highjack highland highlife
highlight highlighter highroad
hightail highway highwayman

home

homebody
homebound
homeboy
homebred
homecoming
homegrown
homeland
homeless
homelike
homemade
homemaker
homeowner
homesick
homespun
homestead
homestretch
hometown
homeward
homework

honey

honeybee
honeycomb
honeycreeper
honeydew
honeyeater
honeymoon
honeysuckle

house

houseboat
housebound
houseboy
housebreak
housebreaker
housebroken
housecleaning
housecoat
housedress
housefather
housefly
houseguest
household
householder
househusband
housewife
housekeep
housekeeper
housekeeping
houseleek
housemaid
houseman
housemate
housemother
houseparent
houseplant
houseroom
housesit
housetop
housewarming
housework

The Compound Words by Camilia Sadik

horse

horseback	**horse**hair	**horse**tail
horsehide	**horse**flesh	**horse**laugh
horseman	**horse**manship	**horse**woman
horseplay	**horse**power	**horse**mint
horseradish	**horse**shoe	**horse**shit
horseweed	**horse**whip	

hot

hotbed	**hot**box	**hot**cakes
hotdog	**hot**foot	**hot**head
hothouse	**hot**line	**hot**link
hotshot	**hot**spot	**Hot**spur
hotwire		

hyper

hyperinflation	**hyper**market	**hyper**irritability
hypersensitive	**hyper**thyroid	**hyper**tension
hyperventilation	**hyper**link	**hyper**text
hypersonic	**hyper**space	**hyper**trophy

Please check your dictionary for more than 150 additional words that begin with **hyper**.

horn

hornbeam	**horn**bill	**horn**pipe
horntail	**horn**worm	**horn**wort

H

hold

holdback **hold**fast **hold**out
holdover **hold**up

hang

hangdog **hang**man **hang**out
hangover

hog

hogback **hog**fish **hog**tie
hogwash

hop

hophead **hop**lite **hop**sacking
hopscotch

hammerhead **hammer**less **hammer**toe
hedgehog **hedge**hop **hedge**row
heelball **heel**piece **heel**tap
helpless **help**mate **help**meet
hemline **hem**lock **hem**stitch
hideaway **hide**bound **hide**out
hindbrain **hind**gut **hind**most
humbug **hum**dinger **hum**drum

hackberry **hack**saw
hailstone **hail**storm

63

hallmark	**hall**way	
heavyset	**heavy**weight	
heatproof	**heat**stroke	
hillside	**hill**top	
hoecake	**hoe**down	
hundredfold	**hundred**weight	
hijacked	**hi**jack	
however	**how**soever	
holyday	**holy**stone	
hookup	**hook**worm	
humpback	**hump**backed	
handyman	**had**dock	**hag**fish
harebrained	**harm**less	**harvest**man
Havelock	**hawk**weed	**hazel**nut
headache	**health**care	**heaven**ward
heirloom	**herring**bone	**her**self
heyday	**him**self	**hip**bone
hobbyhorse	**hob**nail	**ho**bo
hockshop	**hollow**ware	**hitch**hike
hithermost	**hood**wink	**hope**less
hourglass	**hover**craft	**hub**cap
huggermugger	**humble**bee	**humming**bird
hunchback	**hunts**man	**husband**man
heedless	**hee**haw	

H-

half-

half-and-half	**half**-baked	**half**-blood
half-bread	**half**-castle	**half**-cocked
half-cup	**half**-dozen	**half**-gallon
half-glasses	**half**-hour	**half**-length
half-life	**half**-light	**half**-liter
half-moon	**half**-slip	**half**-sole
half-staff	**half**-time	**half**-truth
half-turn	**half**-wit	**half**-crazy

Please check your dictionary for more than 145 additional words that begin with half-.

hands-

hands-down	**hands**-off	**hands**-on
hand-to-hand	**hand**-to-mouth	**hand**-me-down
hand-woven		

hard-

hard-and-fast	**hard**-bitten	**hard**-boiled
hard-core	**hard**-edge	**hard**-hitting

heavy-

heavy-duty	**heavy**-footed	**heavy**-handed
heavy-hearted		

The Compound Words by Camilia Sadik

high-and-mighty	high-class	high-count
high-density	high-definition television	high-energy
high-end	higher-up	high-five
high-flown	high-grade	high-handed
high-hat	high-level	high-minded
high-muck-a-muck	high-occupancy	high-pitched
high-power	high-powered	high-pressure
high-priced	high-rise	high-sounding
high-speed	high-sticking	high-strung
high-tech/hi-tech	high-test	high-tone
high-toned	high-watermark	high-wrought

house-proud	house-raising	house-to-house
house-train		

hot-blooded	hot-button	hot-rod
hot-roll		

hit-and-miss	hit-and-run	hit-or-miss
head-on	head-up	head-to-head

hair-raiser	hair-raising	
hanger-on	hanger-up	

happy-go   happy-lucky

horse-drawn   horse-and-buggy

how-do-you-do   how-to

hawk-eyed   hawk-nosed

habit-forming   hail-fellow   hang-up

have-not   hearing-impaired   hear-to-hear

theat-treat   heave-ho   heaven-sent

heavier-than-air   heebie-jeebies   heed-and-toe

height-to-paper   hell-for-leather   he-man

hen-and-chickens   herky-jerky   hide-and-eek

hepatitis non-A   hepatitis non-B   hip-hop

hog-wild   ho-hum   hoity-toity

hold-and-corner   holier-than-thou   home-care

honky-tonk   horn-rims   hub-and-spoke

Hula-Hoop   human-interest   hundred-percent

hung-up   hunt-and-peck   hunter-gatherer

hurdy-gurdy   hurly-burly   hurry-up

hush-hush   hydra-headed   hunk-dory

⬆ Practice of all the above words: Read the above words aloud slowly as many times as needed until you memorize their spelling.

The Compound Words by Camilia Sadik

✎ Make **11** copies of this page to copy the above compound & hyphenated words that begin with an **H**. Look at each word before you begin to copy it; do not try to guess its spelling:

I

ice

iceberg	**ice**blink	**ice**boat
icebound	**ice**box	**ice**breaker
icecap	**ice**fall	**ice**house
icemaker	**ice**man	**Ice**land

in

inlay	**in**mate	**in**most
input	**in**road	**in**rush
inset	**in**side	**in**sight
insofar	**in**somuch	**in**stall
instate	**in**stead	**in**step
instill	**in**take	**in**tense
intention	**in**tent	**in**tend
inward		

inter

interact	**inter**change	**inter**com
interconnect	**inter**disciplinary	**inter**scholastic
interface	**inter**growth	**inter**link
interlock	**inter**marry	**inter**racial
interrelated	**inter**section	**inter**species

Please check your dictionary for more than 170 additional words that begin with **inter**.

The Compound Words by Camilia Sadik

inkblot	**ink**horn	**ink**stand
innermost	**inner**sole	**inner**spring
outmost	**out**put	**out**ward
outermost		

I-

ill-

ill-advised	**ill**-being	**ill**-bred
ill-boding	**ill**-fated	**ill**-favored
ill-gotten	**ill**-humor	**ill**-mannered
ill-natured	**ill**-starred	**ill**-timed
ill-treat	**ill**-use	**ill**-wisher

in-

in-house	**in**-joke	**in**-law
in-line	**in**-residence	**in**-your-face

I-beam	**inner**-directed	**inter**-American
itty-bitty		

⬆ Practice of all the above words: Read the above words aloud slowly as many times as needed until you memorize their spelling.

✍ Make **two** copies of this page to copy the above compound & hyphenated words that begin with the letter **I**. Look at each word before you begin to copy it; do not try to guess its spelling:

The Compound Words by Camilia Sadik

J

jack

jackass   **jack**boot   **jack**fruit
jackhammer **jack**knife   **jack**leg
jacklight   **jack**pot   **jack**rabbit
jackstay   **jack**straw

jail

jailbait   **jail**bird   **jail**break
jailhouse

jaybird   **jay**hawker   **jay**walk

jawbone   **jaw**breaker
jellybean   **jelly**fish
jetport   **jet**liner
jobholder   **job**less
journeyman **journey**work
joyless   **joy**ride

Jabberwocky **James**town   **jazz**man
Jerkwater   **jig**saw   **jitter**bug
Jockstrap   **johnny**cake   **joint**worm
juicehead   **juke**box   **junk**yard
jurywoman

72

J-

jack-in-the-box **jack**-in-the-pulpit **jack**-of-all-trades **jack**-

Johnny-come-lately **Johnny**-on-the-spot **Johnny**-jump-up **Johnny**-

job-hop **job**-hunt
jet-black **jet**-propelled

jazz-rock **jimmy**-dandy **joint**-stock company
jumping-off-place **jump**-start **jury**-rig
jerry-built

⬆ Practice of all the above words: Read the above words aloud slowly as many times as needed until you memorize their spelling.

The Compound Words by Camilia Sadik

🐌 Make **two** copies of this page to copy the above compound & hyphenated words that begin with a **J**. Look at each word before you begin to copy it; do not try to guess its spelling:

K

key

keyboard   **key**hole   **key**note
keypad   **key**punch   **key**stone
keystroke   **key**word

knock

knockabout   **knock**down   **knock**off
knockout

kick

kickback   **kick**board   **kick**off
kickstand   **kick**boxing

kneecap   **knee**hole   **knee**pad
knotgrass   **knot**hole   **knot**weed

kingmaker   **king**pin
kinsman   **kins**woman
knapsack   **knap**weed
knucklebone   **knuckle**head

keelboat   **keep**sake   **kill**joy
kindhearted   **kitchen**ware   **knick**knack
knifepoint   **knight**hood   **knit**wear

All the Compound Words by Camilia Sadik

K-

know-how	**know**-it-all	**know**-nothing
knee-high	**knee**-jerk	**knee**-sprung

king-size	**king**-sized	
kiss-and-tell	**kiss**-off	
knock-knee	**knock**-down-drag-out	

kick-start	**knuckle**-duster	**kick**-start
kitchen-sink		

⬆ Practice of all the above words: Read the above words aloud slowly as many times as needed until you memorize their spelling.

K

✍ Make **two** copies of this page to copy the above compound & hyphenated words that begin with a **K**. Look at each word before you begin to copy it; do not try to guess its spelling:

The Compound Words by Camilia Sadik

L

lady

ladybug **lady**finger **lady**fish
ladylike **lady**love

land

landfall **land**fill **land**form
landgrave **land**holder **land**lady
landlord **land**less **land**locked
landmark **land**mass **land**owner
landscape **land**slide **land**ward

life

lifeblood **life**boat **life**guard
lifeless **life**like **life**line
lifelong **life**saver **life**style
lifetime **life**work

lock

lockbox **lock**down **lock**jaw
lockout **lock**smith **lock**step
lockup

long

longboat **long**bow **long**hair
longhand **long**headed **long**shoreman

L

longsome   **long**spur   **long**standing
longtime   **long**wise

low

lowball   **low**born   **low**boy
lowbred   **low**brow   **low**down
lowland   **low**life

law

lawbreaker   **law**giver   **law**less
lawmaker   **law**man   **law**suit

lay

layman   **lay**off   **lay**out
layover   **lay**person   **lay**woman

lap

lapboard   **lap**pet   **lap**wing
laptop

log

logbook   **log**normal   **log**roll
logwood

lakefront   **lake**shore   **lake**side
leafhopper   **leaf**let   **leaf**stalk

The Compound Words by Camilia Sadik

leaseback	**lease**hold	**lease**holder
leatherwood	**leather**neck	**leather**head
legman	**leg**room	**leg**work
limelight	**lime**stone	**lime**water
litterbug	**litter**bag	**litter**mate
loadmaster	**load**star	**load**stone
locomotion	**loco**motors	**loco**weed
loudmouth	**loud**mouthed	**loud**speaker
loveless	**love**lock	**love**sick

lamplighter	**lamp**post
latchkey	**latch**string
leadoff	**lead**plant
leastways	**least**wise
leeward	**lee**way
leftover	**left**ward
linebacker	**line**up
linkup	**link**work
lionhearted	**lion**fish
livelong	**live**stock
lodestar	**lode**stone
lookout	**look**up
loosestrife	**loose**stick
lowercase	**lower**most

lunchroom   **lunch**time
lung·ish   **lung**worm

laborsaving   **late**comer   **lazy**bones
leakproof   **leap**frog   **let**down
lickspittle   **lid**less   **liege**man
lengthwise   **like**wise   **ling**berry
lipstick   **little**neck   **livery**man
loanword   **lobster**man   **logger**head
loincloth   **lone**some   **loop**hole
lordship   **lounge**wear   **luck**less
lyrebird   **last**born

L-

life-
life-and-death   **life**-giving   **life**-or-death
life-size   **life**-sized   **life**-support
life-forever   **life**-in

long-
long-chain   **long**-distance   **long**-drawn-out
long-headed   **long**-horned   **long**-lasting
long-lived   **long**-playing   **long**-range
long-sighted   **long**-term   **long**-winded

The Compound Words by Camilia Sadik

look-alike	**look**-in	**look**-see
look-up		

low-density	**low**-end	**low**-grade
low-key	**low**-keyed	**low**-level
low-lying	**low**-minded	**low**-pressure
low-rent	**low**-necked	**low**-pitched
low-rise	**low**-spirited	**low**-tech
low-ticket		

letter-perfect	**letter**-quality	**letter**-size
light-duty	**light**-emitting	**light**-fingered
love-in	**love**-in-a-mist	

lay-up	**lad**-up	**leading**-edge
leg-pull	**lend**-lease	**lickety**-split
lighter-than-air	**like**-minded	**limp**-wrested
lip-synch	**literal**-minded	**local**-area
locker-room	**looking**-glass	**loose**-tongued
loving-kindness		

⬆ Practice of all the above words: Read the above words aloud slowly as many times as needed until you memorize their spelling.

🖎 Make **five** copies of this page to copy the above compound & hyphenated words that begin with an **L**. Look at each word before you begin to copy it; do not try to guess its spelling:

M

mad

madcap · **mad**house · **mad**man
madwoman

main

mainframe · **main**land · **main**mast
mainsail · **main**sheet · **main**spring
mainstay · **main**stream

make

makefast · **make**over · **make**up
makeweight

man

manhood · **man**drake · **man**drill
mangrove · **man**handle · **man**hole
manhunt · **man**like · **man**slaughter
manslayer

master

masterpiece · **master**singer · **master**stroke
masterwork · **master**mind

M

match

matchboard   matchbook   matchless
matchlock   matchmaker   matchstick
matchwood

may

maybe/ may be   mayflower   mayfly
mayflower   mayhap   mayhem
maypop   mayday

mid

Midwest   midlife   midline
midland   midmost   midnight
midpoint   midrange   midrib
midriff   midshipman   midstream
midsummer   midwinter   midterm
midtown   midway   midweek
midwife   midyear

milk

milkfish   milkmaid   milksop
milkweed

mill

millboard   milldam   millhouse
millpond   millstone   millwork

The Compound Words by Camilia Sadik

moon

moonbeam
moonflower
moonrise
moonshine
moonward

mooncalf
moonlight
moonseed
moonstone

moonfish
moonlit
moonset
moonwalk

motor

motorcycle
motorbus
motorman

motorbike
motorcar

motorboat
motorway

mud

mudflow
mudpuppy
mudstone

mudguard
mudroom

mudpack
mudskipper

meadowland
middleman
motherhood
mouthbreeder

meadowlark
middlemost
motherboard
mouthpiece

meadowsweet
middleweight
motherland
mouthpart

meantime
meatball
metalworking
markdown

meanwhile
meathead
metalwork
markup

M

marrowbone
milepost
mindless
minefield
molehill
moneybag
mothball
machinelike
mantelshelf
marshland
mincemeat
mockup
mousetrap
muddleheaded

marrowfat
milestone
mindset
minelayer
moleskin
monkeyshine
mothproof
maidenhair
mapmaker
meltdown
mobcap
moldboard
mouthwash

maidservant
marketplace
dairymaid
mockingbird
mossback
myself

M-

make-believe
make-up work

make-or-break

make-ready

man-about-town
man-days
man-made
man-sized

man-at-arms
man-eater
man-of-war
man-tailored

man-
man-child
man-hour
man-size
man-year

The Compound Words by Camilia Sadik

mind-altering	**mind**-bending	**mind**-blowing
mind-boggling	**mind**-expanding	**mind**-set

made-to-order	**made**-to-measure	**made**-up
middle-of-the-road	**middle**-size	**middle**-sized
mid-rise	**mid**-size	**mid**-sized

mass-market	**mass**-produce
merry-go-round	**merry**-making
medium-size	**medium**-sized
mother-in-law	**mother**-of-pearl
mouth-watering	**mouth**-to-mouth resuscitation

ma-and-pa	**mom**-and-pop	**machine**-readable
maid-in-waiting	**mail**-order house	**many**-sided
master-at-arm	**match**-up	**mater**-of-fact
miller-thumb	**mix**-up	**mock**-up
money-changer	**moon**-blind	**mop**-up
morning-after pill	**moth**-eaten	**mouse**-ear
muck-a-muck	**must**-see	**meat**-and-potatoes
military-industrial complex		

⬆ Practice of all the above words: Read the above words aloud slowly as many times as needed until you memorize their spelling.

✒ Make **five** copies of this page to copy the above compound & hyphenated words that begin with an **M**. Look at each word before you begin to copy it; do not try to guess its spelling:

N

name

nameless   nameplate   namesake
namedropping

needle

needlepoint   needlework   needlewoman
needlefish   needless

new

newcomer   newfound   Newfoundland
newspeak

news

newspaper   newsagent   newsbeat
newsboy   newsgirl   newsbreak
newscast   newsgroup   newsletter
newsmagazine   newsman   newsmonger
newspaperman   newswoman   newsperson
newsprint   newsreader   newsreel
newsroom   newsstand   newsweekly
newswire   newsworthy

night

nightcap   nightclothes   nightdress
nightgown   nighthawk   nightjar
nightlife   nightlong   nightrider
nightshade   nightshirt   nightspot
nightstand   nighttime   nightwalker

N

non

nonaligned   **non**believer   **non**essential
nonfactual   **non**hereditary   **non**native
nonpayment   **non**violent   **non**white
nonprofit

Please check your dictionary for approximately 700 words that begin with "**non**."

nose

noseband   **nose**bleed   **nose**dive
nosegay   **nose**piece

nut

nutcracker   **nut**gall   **nut**hatch
nutmeat   **nut**pick   **nut**shell

notebook   **note**paper   **note**worthy
necktie   **neck**band   **neck**lace

nearby   **near**sighted
network   **net**working
nitpick   **nit**wit
nobleman   **noble**woman
nowadays   **now**here

nailbrush   **narrow**cast   **nation**wide
neighborhood   **nerve**less   **never**theless

91

The Compound Words by Camilia Sadik

newlywed	**nick**name	**no**body
noisemaker	**noon**time	**notch**back
notwithstanding	**nurse**maid	**nursery**man

N-

no-

no-account	**no**-brained	**no**-cal
no-fault	**no**-fly zone	**no**-frills
no-go	**no**-good	**no**-hitter
no-knock	**no**-place	**no**-name
no-nonsense		

non-

non-Catholic	**non**-American	**non**-A hepatitis
non-B hepatitis	**non**-pros	

new-collar	**new**-fashioned	**new**-fangled

nail-biter	**name**-brand	**narrow**-minded
nation-state	**native**-born	**near**-point
neck-rein	**neo**-Freudian	**nerve**-racking
net-winged	**next**-door	**nice**-nellyism
nickel-and-dime	**night**-lamp	**nip**-up
nitty-gritty		

⬆ Practice of all the above words: Read the above words aloud slowly as many times as needed until you memorize their spelling.

✒ Make **three** copies of this page to copy the above compound & hyphenated words that begin with an **N**. Look at each word before you begin to copy it; do not try to guess its spelling:

The Compound Words by Camilia Sadik

O

off

offbeat **off**hand **off**shore
offside **off**spring **off**stage

on

ongoing **on**line **on**rush
onset **on**shore **on**side
onto **on**ward **on**screen
onsite

out

outback **out**balance **out**board
outbound **out**break **out**breed
outcast **out**class **out**come
outcrop **out**cross **out**cry
outdated **out**distance **out**do
outdoors **out**doorswoman **out**doorsman
outdoorsy **out**draw **out**wear
outface **out**fall **out**field
outfit **out**flank **out**flow
outfox **out**gas **out**giving
outgo **out**going **out**growth
outguess **out**gun **out**house
outland **out**lander **out**landish
outlast **out**law **out**lay
outlet **out**lier **out**line

O

outlive	outlook	outlying
outmaneuver	outmatch	outmoded
outmost	outnumber	outpace
outpatient	outperform	outplacement
outpoint	outpost	outpour
output	outrace	outrage
outrageous	outrank	outreach
outride	outrigger	outright
outrun	outsell	outset
outshine	outshoot	outside
outsider	outsight	outsize
outskirt	outsmart	outsole
outsource	outspend	outspoken
outspread	outstanding	outstation
outstay	outstretch	outstrip
outtake	outturn	outvote
outward	outwardly	outwash
outwear	outweigh	outwit
outwork	outworn	

over

overachieve	overact	overactive
overage	overall	overarching
overbalance	overbear	overbearing
overbid	overbite	overblown
overboard	overbook	overbuild

overburden	overbuy	overcall
overcapacity	overcapitalize	overcast
overcharge	overcome	overcommitted
overcompensate	overcrowd	overdevelop
overdo	overdue	overdose
overdraft	overdraw	overdress
overdrive	overdub	overeat
overestimate	overexpose	overextend
overfill	overflow	overgrow
overgrowth	overhand	overhang
overhaul	overhead	overhear
overheat	overindulge	overkill
overland	overlap	overleaf
overleap	overlie	overload
overlook	overlord	overmaster
overmatch	overmuch	overnight
overpass	overpay	overplay
overpopulate	overpower	overprice
overprint	overrate	overreach
overreact	override	overripe
overrule	overrun	overseas
oversee	overseer	oversell
overset	overshadow	overshoe
overshot	oversight	oversimplify
oversize	overskirt	oversleep

O

overspend
overstay
oversubscribe
overthrow
overtop
overturn
overweight
overwrite

overspread
overstep
overtake
overtime
overtrick
overview
overwhelm
overwrought

overstate
overstuff
overtax
overtone
overtrump
overweigh
overwhelming

oilcan

oilcloth

oilstone

oarfish
oatcake

oarlock
oatmeal

oddball
oneself
ownership
outermost

oftentimes
ourselves
oxtail

oldwife
ovenproof
oysterman

O-

off-camera
off-hour
off-limits

off-color
off-key
off-line

off-
off-duty
off-label
off-load

The Compound Words by Camilia Sadik

off-peak	**off**-Broadway	**off**-road
off-putting	**off**-season	**off**-white
off-the-books	**off**-the-cuff	**off**-the-rack
off-the-record	**off**-the-shelf	**off**-the-wall

old-

old-fashioned	**old**-line	**old**-shoe
old-time	**old**-timer	**old**-world

one-

once-over	**one**-fold	**one**-handed
one-horse	**one**-man-band	**one**-night-stand
one-on-one	**one**-to-one	**one**-piece
one-shot	**one**-sided	**one**-step
one-time	**one**-track	**one**-two
one-up	**one**-way	**one**-woman

out-

out-and-out	**out**-front	**out**-group
out-migrate	**out**-of-body	**out**-of-bonds
out-of-date	**out**-of-doors	**out**-of-pocket
out-of-sight	**out**-of-state	**out**-of-the-way

on-board	**on**-coming	**on**-the-job
oven-ready	**over**-the-counter	**okey**-doke

⬆ Practice of all the above words: Read the above words aloud slowly as many times as needed until you memorize their spelling.

✎ Make **seven** copies of this page to copy the above compound & hyphenated words that begin with an **O**. Look at each word before you begin to copy it; do not try to guess its spelling:

P

paint

paintball   **paint**box   **paint**brush
paintwork

pan

panache   **pan**cake   **pan**handler
pantry

paper

paperback   **paper**less   **paper**weight
paperwork

pass

passbook   **Pass**over   **pass**port
password

pay

payback   **pay**load   **pay**master
payout   **pay**phone   **pay**roll

photo

photocell   **photo**copier   **photo**copy
photoelectric   **photo**graph   **photo**graphic
photojournalism   **photo**sensitive   **photo**synthesis

P

pin

pinball · pincushion · pinhead
pinhole · pinpoint · pinprick

play

playback · playbill · playboy
playground · playgroup · playhouse
playmate · playpen · playroom
playschool · plaything · playtime
playwright

post

postbag · postbox · postcard
postcode · postdoctoral · postgraduate
posthumous · postman · postmark
postmaster · postmistress · postmodern
postmodernism · postpone · postscript

pot

potboiler · pothole · potholing
potluck · potshot

psycho

psychoanalysis · psychoanalyst · psychodrama
psychological · psychometric · psychopath
psychopathology · psychotherapy

push

pushbike	**push**chair	**push**over
pushpin		

painkiller	**pain**less	**pains**taking
peacekeeping	**peace**maker	**peace**time
penchant	**pen**knife	**pen**manship
pickaxe	**pick**pocket	**pick**up
pigskin	**pig**swill	**pig**tail
plainchant	**plain**song	**plain**tiff
powerboat	**power**house	**power**less

pacemaker	**pace**setter
palpate	**pal**try
parkland	**park**way
pathfinder	**path**way
patrolman	**patrol**woman
pawnbroker	**pawn**shop
peashooter	**pea**cock
peppercorn	**pepper**mint
piecemeal	**piece**work
pinstripe	**pin**wheel
pineapple	**pine**wood
pipedream	**pipe**line

pitfall
plasterboard
ploughman
poleax
policeman
popcorn
portfolio
prizefight
Pullman
padlock
pantsuit
partnership
pasteboard
peephole
piggyback
pillowcase
plughole
pointless
poolside
pornographic
pressman
proofread
punchbowl

pithead
plasterwork
ploughshare
polecat
policewoman
popgun
porthole
prizewinner
pullover
pageboy
pantyhose
partygoer
pastureland
peerless
pikestaff
pipsqueak
plywood
policyholder
poorhouse
praiseworthy
priceless
puffball
purposeless

palmtop
parenthood
passionless
patchwork
pennyworth
pillbox
pitchfork
pocketbook
ponytail
poppycock
pratfall
priesthood
pumpkin
pussyfoot

The Compound Words by Camilia Sadik

P-

part-
part-time   **part**-timer   **part**-way
part-work

post-
post-date   **post**-free   **post**-haste
post-industrial   **post**-natal   **post**-operative
post-paid   **post**-traumatic   **post**-war

pull-
pull-down   **pull**-out   **pull**-tab
pull-up

play-acting   **play**-by-play   **play**-off
push-button   **push**-start   **push**-up
put-down   **put**-on   **put**-upon

penny-farthing   **penny**-pinching
pen-name   **pen**-pusher
pick-and-mix   **pick**-me-up
picture-perfect   **picture**-postcard
pitch-black   **pitch**-dark
pop-eyed   **pop**-up

press-gang   **press**-up
profit-making   **profit**-sharing
punch-drunk   **punch**-up

paid-up   **pall**-bearer   **pan**-fry
panic-stricken   **paper**-thin   **parents**-in-law
parish-pump   **parrot**-fashion   **passer**-by
party-pooper   **pass**-fail   **pay**-off
peace-loving   **pea**-green   **pear**-shaped
pebble-dash   **pencil**-pusher   **phone**-in
photo-fit   **pigeon**-hole   **pig**-headed
pile-up   **pinch**-hit   **pint**-sized
pin-up   **pipe**-cleaner   **piss**-up
pistol-whip   **pocket**-sized   **point**-blank
poker-faced   **pony**-trekking   **pot**-bellied
potty-train   **poverty**-stricken   **power**-sharing
president-elect   **price**-fixing   **prize**-giving
problem-solving   **public**-spirited   **pump**-priming
pure-bred   **purpose**-built

⬆ Practice of all the above words: Read the above words aloud slowly as many times as needed until you memorize their spelling.

The Compound Words by Camilia Sadik

🖎 Make **six** copies of this page to copy the above compound & hyphenated words that begin with a **P**. Look at each word before you begin to copy it; do not try to guess its spelling:

Q

quick

quicklime   **quick**sand   **quick**silver

quickstep

quarterback   **quarter**deck   **quarter**master

quarrelsome   **quay**side

Q-

quick-fire   **quick**-tempered   **quick**-witted

quarter-final

⬆ Practice of all the above words: Read the above words aloud slowly as many times as needed until you memorize their spelling.

✏ Copy these compound words and hyphenated words that begin with a **Q**. Look at each word before you begin to copy it; do not try to guess the spelling of these words:

quicklime	quicksand	quicksilver	quickstep
_____	_____	_____	_____
quarterback	quarterdeck	quartermaster	quarrelsome
_____	_____	_____	_____
quayside	quick-fire	quick-witted	quick-tempered
_____	_____	_____	_____
quarter-final			
_____	_____	_____	_____

R

rag

ragbag   **rag**out   **rag**tag
ragtime

rail

railcar   **rail**head   **rail**road
railway

rain

rainbow   **rain**coat   **rain**drop
rainfall   **rain**forest   **rain**proof
rainstorm   **rain**water

ring

ringleader   **ring**master   **ring**side
ringworm

ram

rampage   **ram**pant   **ram**part
ramrod   **ram**shackle

red

redcurrant   **red**den   **red**dish
redhead   **red**neck   **red**olent
redskin   **red**wood

R

road

roadblock   **road**house   **road**runner
roadside   **road**way   **road**work
roadworthy

run

runabout   **run**around   **run**away
runway

racecourse   **race**horse   **race**track
radioactive   **radio**carbon   **radio**therapy
rearguard   **rear**most   **rear**ward
retroactive   **retro**fit   **retro**grade
roughcast   **rough**neck   **rough**shod

restless   **rest**room
riddance   **rid**den
riverfront   **river**side
rollback   **roll**over
rooftop   **root**less
rosebud   **rose**wood
roundabout   **round**worm
rowboat   **row**lock

The Compound Words by Camilia Sadik

racquetball · **raga**muffin · **ran**sack
ratepayer · **rattle**snake · **raw**hide
reckless · **regard**less · **relent**less
remorseless · **rib**cage · **rich**ness
rickshaw · **rifle**man · **right**ward
rimless · **rip**cord · **roust**about
rubberneck · **ruck**sack · **rudder**less
rustproof

R-

red-

red-blooded · **red**-brick · **red**-eye
red-faced · **red**-handed · **red**-hot

right-

right-angled · **right**-hand · **right**-handed
right-minded · **right**-on · **right**-wing
right-winger

roll-

roll-call · **roll**-on · **roll**-out
roll-up

R

round-eyed   **round**-shouldered   **round**-table
round-the-clock   **round**-up

run-off   **run**-of-the-mill   **run**-through
run-up

radio-controlled   **radio**-telephone
razor-sharp   **razor**-thin
ready-made   **ready**-to-wear
rear-end   **rear**-view
rip-off   **rip**-roaring
rock-bottom   **rock**-hard
rough-and-ready   **rough**-hewn
run-down   **run**-in

rake-off   **ram**-raiding   **rapid**-fire
read-out   **real**-life   **rent**-free
ring-fence   **risk**-taking   **role**-play
room-mate   **rose**-colored   **rubber**stamp
runner-up

⬆ Practice of all the above words: Read the above words aloud slowly as many times as needed until you memorize their spelling.

111

The Compound Words by Camilia Sadik

🐌 Make **four** copies of this page to copy the above compound & hyphenated words that begin with an **R**. Look at each word before you begin to copy it; do not try to guess its spelling:

S

sales/ sale
salesman
salesmanship
salesperson
salesroom
saleroom

sand
sandbag
sandbank
sandbar
sandblast
sandbox
sandcastle
sandman
sandpaper
sandpiper

school
schoolboy
schoolchild
schooldays
schoolgirl
schoolhouse
schoolmaster
schoolmistress
schoolmate
schoolteacher

sea
seabird
seaboard
seaborne
seafarer
seafaring
seafood
seagoing
seagull
sealant
seaman
seamanship
seaplane
seaport
seascape
seashell
seashore
seasick
seaside
season
seaway
seaweed
seaworthy

The Compound Words by Camilia Sadik

share
sharecropper   **share**holder   **share**holding
shareware

ship
shipboard   **ship**builder   **ship**load
shipmate   **ship**shape   **ship**wreck
shipyard

shoe
shoehorn   **shoe**lace   **shoe**maker
shoeshine   **shoe**string

short
shortbread   **short**cake   **short**coming
shorthand

show
showcase   **show**down   **show**girl
showground   **show**man   **show**manship
showpiece   **show**place   **show**room
Showtime   **show**down

sick
sickbay   **sick**bed   **sick**out
sickroom

side

sideboard sidecar sidekick
sidelight sideline sidelong
sideshow sidestep sideswipe
sidetrack sidewalk sideways

sky

skycap skydiving skylark
skylight skyline skyrocket
skyscraper skywards

slip

slippage slipshod slipstream
slipway

snow

snowball snowdrift snowdrop
snowfall snowfield snowflake
snowline snowman snowmobile
snowshoe snowstorm

some

somebody someday somehow
someone someplace something
sometimes someway somewhat
somewhere

song
songbird   songbook   songstress
songwriter   songwriting

space
spacecraft   spaceman   spaceship
spacesuit   spacewoman

sports
sportscast   sportscaster   sportsman
sportsmanlike   sportsmanship   sportsperson
sportswear

stand
standout   standpipe   standpoint
standstill

star
starboard   starfish   starless
starlight

state/ states
statewide   stateless   stateroom
stateside   statesman   statesmanlike
statesmanship

step

stepbrother stepchild stepdaughter
stepfather stepmother stepsister
stepson stepladder

stock

stockbroker stockholder stockman
stockpile stockroom stocktaking
stockyard

stone

stonemason stonewall stoneware
stonewashed stonework

stop

stopcock stopgap stopover
stoppage stopwatch

store

storefront storehouse storekeeper
storeroom

sun

sunbathe sunbeam sunbelt
sunburn Sunday sundial
sundown sundress sundry
sunflower sunglasses sunhat
sunlamp sunless sunlight
sunrise sunroof sunroom
sunscreen sunset sunshade

The Compound Words by Camilia Sadik

sunshine	**sun**spot	**sun**stroke
suntan	**sun**trap	

super

superabundance	**super**annuated	**super**annuation
supercharged	**super**conductivity	**super**computer
superconductor	**super**ego	**super**glue
superhero	**super**highway	**super**human
superimpose	**super**intend	**super**intendent
superman	**super**market	**super**model
supernatural	**super**power	**super**script
supersonic	**super**star	**super**store
superstructure	**super**tanker	**super**visor
superwoman		

sweat

sweatband	**sweat**pants	**sweat**shirt
sweatshop		

sandpit	**sand**stone	**sand**storm
scoreboard	**score**card	**score**less
shopkeeper	**shop**lifting	**shop**worn
skinflint	**skin**head	**skin**tight
sleepless	**sleep**over	**sleep**walk
slowcoach	**slow**down	**slow**poke
smallholder	**small**holding	**small**pox

S

smokeless	smokescreen	smokestack
softball	software	softwood
soundless	soundproof	soundtrack
southbound	southpaw	southwards
spellbinding	spellbound	spellchecker
staircase	stairway	stairwell
steamboat	steamroller	steamship
storyboard	storybook	storyteller
straightaway	straightforward	straightjacket
streetcar	streetwalker	streetwise
strongbox	stronghold	strongman
sweetbread	sweetheart	sweetmeat
switchback	switchblade	switchboard

sailboard	sailboat
sawdust	sawmill
screenplay	screenwriter
screwball	screwdriver
seamless	seamstress
seedbed	seedless
shamefaced	shameless
sheepdog	sheepskin
shellfire	shellfish
sightless	sightseeing
signboard	signpost

The Compound Words by Camilia Sadik

silverfish	silverware	
slapdash	slapstick	
snakebite	snakeskin	
snapdragon	snapshot	
soapbox	soapstone	
spearhead	spearmint	
speedboat	speedway	
spokesman	spokesperson	
spotless	spotlight	
springboard	springtime	
stagecoach	stagehand	
steelworker	steelworks	
steeplechase	steeplejack	
stillbirth	stillborn	
swimsuit	swimwear	
swordfish	swordsman	
sackcloth	saddlebag	safeguard
sagebrush	saltbox	sandalwood
saucepan	scatterbrain	Scotland
scrapbook	scriptwriter	scumbag
scuttlebutt	searchlight	seersucker
senseless	selfless	serviceman
setback	sexless	shakedown
shamrock	shapeless	sharpshooter
shiftless	shirtsleeve	shitless

S

shoreline	shotgun	shuttlecock
signalman	silkworm	simpleton
sisterhood	skateboard	sketchbook
skidpan	skullcap	slattern
slaughterhouse	sledgehammer	slingshot
snuffbox	soulless	sourdough
southernmost	spadework	speakeasy
speakerphone	speechless	spendthrift
spillover	spineless	spiritless
splashdown	spoilsport	sponsorship
spreadsheet	stableman	stainless
stakeholder	stalemate	stallholder
steadfast	stereotype	stewardship
stickleback	stickpin	stingray
stowaway	stranglehold	strapless
strawberry	streamline	stubborn
studentship	stuntman	suchlike
suitcase	summertime	strikeout
striptease	sweepstake	

S-

second-class	second-degree	second-second-guess
second-hand	second-rate	second-string

self-

self-absorbed	self-access	self-adhesive
self-appointed	self-appraisal	self-assembly
self-assertive	self-assessment	self-assured
self-awareness	self-catering	self-centered
self-confessed	self-congratulations	self-confident
self-conscious	self-contradictory	self-contained
self-control	self-criticism	self-deception
self-defeating	self-defense	self-denial
self-deprecating	self-destruct	self-destruction
self-determination	self-discipline	self-doubt
self-drive	self-educated	self-effacing
self-employed	self-esteem	self-evident
self-examination	self-explanatory	self-expression
self-fulfilling	self-fulfillment	self-government
self-help	self-image	self-important
self-imposed	self-induced	self-indulgent
self-inflicted	self-interest	self-made
self-mutilation	self-opinionated	self-pity
self-portrait	self-preservation	self-possessed
self-proclaimed	self-raising	self-reliant
self-respect	self-respecting	self-restraint
self-righteous	self-rule	self-sacrifice
self-same	self-satisfied	self-seeking
self-service	self-serving	self-starter

S

self-styled   self-sufficient   self-supporting
self-taught   self-worth

short-change   short-circuit   short-handed
short-haul   short-lived   short-order
short-range   short-sighted   short-staffed
short-stay   short-term

six-figure   six-gun   six-pack
six-shooter   six-former

soft-boiled   soft-hearted   soft-pedal
soft-soap   soft-spoken

south-east   south-easterly   south-eastern
south-eastwards   south-west   south-westerly
south-western   south-westwards

sun-baked   sun-dried   sun-drenched
sun-up   sun-worshipper

set-aside   set-to   set-up
shut-eye   shut-in   shut-out
single-breasted   single-decker   single-handed

123

The Compound Words by Camilia Sadik

small-minded	small-scale	small-time
snow-capped	snow-covered	snow-white
stand-alone	stand-by	stand-up

shake-out	shake-up
shoulder-high	shoulder-length
show-off	show-stopper
side-on	side-saddle
sky-blue	sky-high
slap-happy	slap-up
slip-up	slip-on
slow-witted	slow-worm
soul-destroying	soul-searching
split-level	split-second
spring-clean	spring-loaded
stage-manage	stage-struck
star-crossed	star-studded
stick-in-the-mud	stick-on
stir-crazy	stir-fry
stock-in-trade	stock-still
straight-faced	straight-laced
store-bought	store-brand
strike-bound	strike-breaker
strong-arm	strong-minded
sure-fire	sure-footed

S

sweet-and-sour   sweet-talk
see-saw   see-through
sell-off   sell-out
send-off   send-up

saber-rattling   saddle-sore   say-so
school-leaver   scot-free   screwed-up
screw-top   scuba-diving   sea-green
sending-off   shadow-box   sharp-eyed
shatter-proof   shell-shocked   ship-to-shore
shoot-out   shop-bought   shrink-wrapped
sight-read   silk-screen   simple-minded
sister-in-law   sit-up   skew-whiff
skin-deep   skinny-dipping   slam-dunk
slate-grey   slave-driver   small-town
smash-and-grab   smoke-free   smooth-talking
snarl-up   so-called   son-in-law
sort-out   spine-chilling   spin-off
starry-eyed   start-up   stay-at-home
step-parent   standard-bearer   stake-out
stiff-necked   stomach-ache   stony-faced
stop-go   stretcher-bearer storm-tossed
stuck-up   sugar-coat   supply-side
surface-to-air   swearing-in

⬆ Practice of all the above words: Read the above words aloud slowly as many times as needed until you memorize their spelling.

The Compound Words by Camilia Sadik

🐭 Make **15** copies of this page to copy the above compound & hyphenated words that begin with an **S**. Look at each word before you begin to copy it; do not try to guess its spelling:

T

table

tablecloth   **table**spoon   **table**ware

tail

tailback   **tail**board   **tail**bone
tailcoat   **tail**gate   **tail**piece
tailpipe   **tail**spin   **tail**wind

tea

teacake   **tea**cart   **tea**cup
teapot   **tea**spoon   **tea**time

there

thereabouts   **there**after   **there**by
therefore   **there**in   **there**of
thereon   **there**upon

thunder

thunderbolt   **thunder**clap   **thunder**cloud
thunderstorm   **thunder**struck

time

timekeeper   **time**keeping   **time**less
timeout   **time**piece   **time**server

127

All the Compound Words by Camilia Sadik

| timescale | timeshare | timetable |

tooth
| toothache | toothbrush | toothless |
| toothpaste | toothpick | |

top
topcoat	topknot	topless
topmost	topnotch	topsoil
topspin		

turn
turnabout	turnaround	turncoat
turnkey	turnout	turnover
turnpike	turnstile	turntable

type
typecast	typeface	typescript
typesetter	typewriter	typewriting
typewritten		

thoroughbred	thoroughfare	thoroughgoing
thumbnail	thumbscrew	thumbtack
tiebreak	tiebreaker	tiepin
toecap	toehold	toenail
touchdown	touchline	touchstone

T

treeless · treelike · treetop
troublemaker · troubleshooter · troublesome
turbocharger · turbojet · turboprop

takeaway · takeover
teammate · teamwork
tenfold · tenpin
threadbare · threadworm
threefold · threesome
throughout · throughput
throwaway · throwback
tidemark · tidewater
tightrope · tightwad
tinfoil · tinplate
tireless · tiresome
townscape · township
tramlines · tramway
tumbledown · tumbleweed
twofold · twosome

tactless · tallboy · tapeworm
taproot · taxpayer · teardrop
tenderloin · textbook · thanksgiving
theatergoer · themselves · thenceforth
thickset · thistledown · thoughtless

thruway	**thy**self	**tinder**box
tiptoe	**toad**stool	**toast**master
tollbooth	**tomb**stone	**tone**less
torchlight	**tow**path	**towns**people
tradesman	**trade**mark	**trail**blazer
trapdoor	**tread**mill	**trend**setter
tribesman	**trip**wire	**trolley**bus
troopship	**truck**load	**trustee**ship
trustworthy	**tune**less	**turtle**neck

T-

tax-

tax-deductible	**tax**-exempt	**tax**-free
tax-payer		

tight-

tight-fisted	**tight**-fitting	**tight**-knit
tight-lipped	**tight**-rope	**tight**-ward

time-

time-consuming	**time**-honored	**time**-saving
time-worn		

top-

top-class	**top**-down	**top**-flight
top-grossing	**top**-heavy	**top**-level
top-ranking	**top**-of-the-range	**top**-rated
top-up		

T

two-

two-bit	**two**-dimensional	**two**-edged
two-faced	**two**-handed	**two**-piece
two-ply	**two**-seater	**two**-time
two-tone	**two**-way	

take-home	**take**-off	**take**-up
third-class	**third**-degree	**third**-rate
tie-dye	**tie**-in	**tie**-up
tongue-in-cheek	**tongue**-tied	**tongue**-twister
touch-and-go	**touch**-tone	**touch**-type

tip-off	**tip**-top	
true-blue	**true**-life	
turn-off	**turn**-up	

tailor-made	**talking**-to	**tape**-record
telling-off	**term**-time	**terror**-stricken
thick-skinned	**thin**-skinned	**thought**-provoking
throw-in	**tin**-opener	**title**-holder
toffee-nosed	**toilet**-train	**tone**-deaf
toss-up	**touchy**-freely	**tractor**-trailer
travel-sick	**trigger**-happy	**try**-out
tub-thumping	**tumble**-dryer	**twenty**-first

⬆ Practice of all the above words: Read the above words aloud slowly as many times as needed until you memorize their spelling.

All the Compound Words by Camilia Sadik

🐌 Make **six** copies of this page to copy the above compound & hyphenated words that begin with a **T**. Look at each word before you begin to copy it; do not try to guess its spelling:

U

underachieve
underbid
undercharge
underclasswoman
undercover
underdeveloped
underemployed
underfed
undergo
undergrowth
underlie
undermine
underpants
underpin
underrate
undersecretary
underside
understaffed
understate
undertake
undertone
underutilized
underway

underarm
underbrush
underclass
underclothes
undercurrent
underdog
underestimate
underfoot
undergraduate
underhand
underline
undernourished
underpass
underplay
underscore
undersell
undersized
understand
understatement
undertaker
undertow
undervalue
underwear

under
underbelly
undercarriage
underclassman
undercoat
undercut
underdone
underexpose
undergarment
underground
underlay
underlying
underpaid
underpay
underprivileged
undersea
undershirt
undersold
understanding
understudy
undertaking
underused
underwater
underweight

The Compound Words by Camilia Sadik

underwent	**under**whelming	**under**world
underwrite	**under**writer	

up

upbeat	upbraid	upbringing
upcoming	update	upfront
upgrade	uphill	uphold
upholster	upkeep	upland
uplift	uplifted	uplifting
uppity	upraised	upright
uprising	upriver	uproar
uproot	upscale	upsetting
upshot	upside	upstage
upstairs	upstanding	upstart
upstate	upstream	upsurge
upswing	uptake	uptight
uptown	uptrend	upturn
upward	upwind	

uppercut	**upper**most
useless	**utter**most

U-

up-

up-and-coming	**up**-country	**up**-tempo
up-to-the-minute		

under-the-counter	**user**-friendly

134

👁 Make **three** copies of this page to copy the above compound & hyphenated words that begin with a **U**. Look at each word before you begin to copy it; do not try to guess its spelling:

The Compound Words by Camilia Sadik

V

video
videoconferencing   **video**disc   **video**phone
videotape

voiceless   **voice**mail   **voice**over
viewfinder   **view**point
valueless   **vine**yard   **volley**ball
voltmeter   **vouch**safe

V-

vice-president

⬆ Practice of all the above words: Read the above words aloud slowly as many times as needed until you memorize their spelling.

✍ Copy these compound words and hyphenated words that begin with a **V**. Look at words before you begin to copy them and do not try to guess their spelling:

videodisc	videophone	videotape	voiceless
_____	_____	_____	_____
voicemail	voiceover	viewfinder	viewpoint
_____	_____	_____	_____
valueless	vineyard	volleyball	voltmeter
_____	_____	_____	_____
vouchsafe	vice-president	videoconferencing	
_____	_____	_____	_____

W

walk
walkabout walkman walkout
walkover walkway

war
warhead warhorse warlike
warlock warlord warpath
warship wartime warthog
warfare

wash
washbasin washboard washcloth
washout washroom washstand

watch
watchband watchdog watchmaker
watchman watchtower watchword

water
waterbed watercolor watercourse
watercress waterfall waterfowl
waterfront waterhole waterline
waterlogged watermark watermelon

The Compound Words by Camilia Sadik

watermill	waterproof	watershed
waterside	waterspout	watertight
waterway	waterwheel	waterworks

way
wayfarer	waylay	wayside
wayward		

weather
weatherboard	weathercock	weatherman
weatherproof	weathervane	

week
weekday	weekend	weeklong
weeknight		

wheel
wheelbarrow	wheelbase	wheelchair
wheelhouse	wheelwright	

where
whereabouts	whereas	whereby
wherefore	wherein	whereof
whereupon		

white
whitebait	whiteboard	whitecaps

w

Whitehall　　**white**wall　　**white**wash

whole

wholegrain　　**whole**hearted　　**whole**sale
wholesaling　　**whole**some

wind

windbag　　**wind**break　　**wind**cheater
windfall　　**wind**lass　　**wind**less
windmill　　**wind**pipe　　**wind**screen
windshield　　**wind**sock　　**wind**surfer
windsurfing　　**wind**swept　　**wind**ward

with

withdraw　　**with**drawn　　**with**hold
within　　**with**out　　**with**stand
withstand

wood

woodblock　　**wood**carving　　**wood**chuck
woodcock　　**wood**cut　　**wood**cutter
woodland　　**wood**louse　　**wood**man
woodpecker　　**wood**shed　　**wood**wind
woodwork　　**wood**worm

The Compound Words by Camilia Sadik

work

workbench	workbook	workday
workfare	workforce	workhorse
workhouse	workload	workman
workmanlike	workmanship	workmate
workout	workplace	workroom
worksheet	workshop	workstation
worktop	workweek	

waistband	waistcoat	waistline
whatever	whatnot	whatsoever
wildfire	wildfowl	wildlife
wingless	wingspan	wingtips
womanhood	womankind	womenfolk
wallflower	wallpaper	
wardrobe	wardroom	
warehouse	warehousing	
wastebasket	wasteland	
webbed	webmaster	
weightless	weightlifting	
westbound	westwards	
wetback	wetland	
whirlpool	whirlwind	
windowless	windowpane	
winnow	winsome	

W

wireless   wiretapping
wordless   wordplay
worthless   worthwhile

wagtail   wedlock   weaverbird
weighbridge   wellspring   welterweight
westernmost   whalebone   whenever
whetstone   whichever   Whitsun
whoever   whomever   whomsoever
whosoever   wickerwork   wicketkeeper
widespread   widowhood   wintertime
wisecrack   wishbone   witchcraft
witless   wolfhound   wonderland
woodsman   worldwide   wormwood
worrywart   wristwatch   wrongdoing

W-

water-borne   water-repellent   water-
water-ski   water-resistant

white-bread   white-collar   white-
white-hot   white-out   white-hall
                                    white-tie

The Compound Words by Camilia Sadik

world-beater   **world**-class   **world**-famous   **world**-weary

write-down   **write**-in   **write**-off   **write**-up

walk-in   **walk**-on   **walk**-up
warm-blooded   **warm**-hearted   **warm**-up
well-being   **well**-groomed   **well**-wisher

waist-deep   **waist**-high
wall-mounted   **wall**-to-wall
whistle-blower   **whistle**-stop
wide-eyed   **wide**-ranging
wind-blown   **wind**-up
work-shy   **work**-to-rule
wrong-foot   **wrong**-headed

war-torn   **washing**-up   **way**-out
wafer-thin   **week**-kneed   **weather**-beaten
week-long   **weight**-in   **wheeler**-dealer
whip-round   **whole**-wheat   **window**-shopping
wire-cutters   **witch**-hunt   **word**-perfect
worldly-wise   **worm**-eaten   **worst**-case

⬆ Read the above words aloud slowly as many times as needed until you memorize them.

👁 Make **six** copies of this page to copy the above compound & hyphenated words that begin with a **W**. Look at each word before you begin to copy it; do not try to guess its spelling:

The Compound Words by Camilia Sadik

Y

yard

yardage   **yard**man   **yard**master
yardarm   **yard**stick

yellow

yellowbird   **yellow**cake   **yellow**hammer
Yellowstone   **yellow**tail

yachtsman   **yachts**woman

yearbook   **young**ling   **your**self

Y-

year-end   **year**-long   **year**-round

yellow-bellied   **yes**-man   **you**-all

⬆ Read the above words aloud slowly as many times as needed until you memorize them.

🖎 Make a copy of page 146 to copy the above words that begin with a **Y**. Look at each word before you begin to copy it.

Z

zoo

zookeeper   zoological   zoogeography
zoophobia   zooplankton

zebrawood   Zululand

Z-

zero-

zero-based   zero-rated   zero-coupon
zero-sum

⬆ Practice of all the above words: Read the above words aloud slowly as many times as needed until you memorize their spelling.

The Compound Words by Camilia Sadik

🐌 Copy the above compound & hyphenated words that begin with a **Z**. Look at each word before you begin to copy it; do not try to guess its spelling:

> Know that the **26** English letters produce over **90** sounds we call phonics, which are spelled in more than **180** ways we call spelling patterns.

Phonics-based Spelling Books by Camilia Sadik

Book 1: *Learn to Spell 500 Words a Day* (6 volumes: A, E, I, O, U, Consonants)
Vowels are inconsistent, they rule English, and they cannot be avoided. In this book, each vowel is dissected and isolated in a volume. The eight consonants c, g, h, q, s, x, w, and y are also inconsistent; and they are isolated in a volume. Each lesson begins with a spelling rule, followed by a list of the words that follow that rule, followed by comprehensive and detailed practice lessons, and students are asked to read aloud to memorize the spelling of hundreds of words at a time. This book is for the intermediate level, ideal for grades 4-12 and for adult learners.

Book 2: *100 Spelling Rules*
Each spelling rule in this book is followed by a list of nearly all the words that follow it. Advanced students learn to spell hundreds of words from this book. Sadik's books are cumulative, and the book *100 Spelling Rules* is a book for the advance level.

Book 3: *Read Instantly* - A book to teach phonics
This book is to teach phonics, and in it lies the groundwork for learning the rules that govern phonics. Anyone capable of learning the ABC's is guaranteed to learn to read from this book. Each vowel is dissected and isolated in a chapter in the second half of this book. Parents can now teach reading before sending kids to schools. This book is for beginners, but all learners need to start with it to learn phonics in a brand-new way.

Book 4: *The Compound Words* (7,000 Compound and Hyphenated Words)
Unlike looking up words in a dictionary, over 5,000 compound words and 2,000 hyphenated words are isolated in this book, grouped alphabetically, colored, and prepared for adults and children to read and learn. As in "rustproof," a compound word is composed of two or more words. As in "face-to-face," a hyphenated word is made of the two or more words, separated by hyphens.

Book 5: *Teachers' Guide*
This guide is for teachers, parents, or adult learners. It contains explanations of the methodology and the symbols and concepts used in the books. It contains dyslexia solutions, spelling tests, and more. *Read more* SpellingRules.com

How to purchase books by Camilia Sadik

SpellingRules.com   Amazon.com   Bookstores Worldwide

About the Author

Linguist Camilia Sadik spent 15 years intensely dissecting English, discovering over 100 spelling rules, applying the rules in 600 phonics-based spelling lessons, class-testing her discoveries and preparing learning books for children and adults to read and spell hundreds of words at a time. The 30 unique learning features in Sadik's book make learning to read and spell inescapable. Sadik worked hard to make spelling easy and possible for all ages and all types of learners. In addition, Sadik found out that dyslexia in spelling and in writing letters in reverse ends, after learning to spell and after slowing down to write words slowly.

Sadik saw the details of English sounds and their various spelling patterns and used that in easy-to-use vowels and consonants books. See these examples:

  The vowel **A** has 5 sounds that are spelled in 12 ways.

  The vowel **E** has 7 sounds that are spelled in 17 ways.

  The vowel **I** has 8 sounds that are spelled in 19 ways.

  The vowel **O** has 12 sounds that are spelled in 20 ways.

  The vowel **U** has 6 sounds that are spelled in 28 ways.

  Eight **consonants** have 50 sounds that are spelled in 60 ways.

Academically, Sadik earned a BA in Philosophy from WSU and an MA in Applied Linguistics from SDSU. In addition, Sadik earned California Teaching Credentials and is certified in teaching ABE and ESL. Before writing books, Sadik spent over 10 years reading the best of the world's literature.

©1997 Camilia Sadik

All rights reserved. Camilia Sadik patented each new spelling rule she discovered. Printed in the United States of America, and except as permitted under the United States Copyright Act of 1976. No part of this publication may be reproduced or distributed in any form or by any means, or stored in a database retrieval system, without prior written permission of the publisher.

www.ingramcontent.com/pod-product-compliance
Lightning Source LLC
Chambersburg PA
CBHW060514300426
44112CB00017B/2669